ARRIVA MERSEYSIDE BUSES

SIMON ACKERS

AMBERLEY

First published 2024

Amberley Publishing
The Hill, Stroud
Gloucestershire, GL5 4EP

www.amberley-books.com

ISBN 978 1 3981 2107 2 (print)
ISBN 978 1 3981 2108 9 (ebook)

British Library Cataloguing in Publication Data.
A catalogue record for this book is available from the British Library.

Origination by Amberley Publishing.
Printed in the UK.

Introduction

The Arriva name and logo have been a familiar sight on the sides of buses in Merseyside since 1998. As with most bus groups there is a history, which I will summarise briefly but it could easily have a book to itself. In 1986 Ribble Motor Services was split up at deregulation and the Merseyside, West Lancashire, and Wigan garages traded as North Western. These operations were sold to Drawlane in 1988, and four years later in 1992 were sold again to British Bus. In 1996 British Bus was bought by the Cowie Group, who renamed as Arriva in 1997. In 1998 North Western, under which the buses had continued to operate, was rebranded as Arriva North West.

At this time Arriva was not the major bus operator in the Merseyside area, operating out of a split depot site in Bootle and having other routes penetrating into the area from their Runcorn, Skelmersdale, and Warrington depots. It was the purchase of MTL Trust Holdings in early 2000 that catapulted them to the network dominance that remains at the time of preparing this book in 2023. In a deal valued at approximately £34.7 million, as well as taking on £50 million of debt, Arriva got 2,500 staff, 970 vehicles, and six main depots. And it is at that point that this book begins to tell the Arriva Merseyside story. Without getting into the complications of O licences and service registrations, it is that point when 'Arriva Merseyside' really began.

Overnight in February 2000 all of the MTL vehicles received 'Arriva serving Merseyside' logos, and then the hard work began. Something that MTL had struggled with was the age profile of their fleet, and Arriva acquired ex-PTE Leyland Atlanteans and ex-London Leyland Titans that were nearly twenty years old (some even older). The fleet, on the whole, was not renumbered unless there was a specific clash, and the MTL numbering system remained until the last buses were withdrawn. Repaints of vehicles began almost instantly, so quickly in fact that some of the buses in Gillmoss had to be repainted back into red and cream following the decision to sell. There was no direct instruction as such to sell Gillmoss specifically, but as part of the acquisition the Monopolies and Mergers Commission stated that a percentage of the new Merseyside operation needed to be sold to prevent Arriva holding a monopoly in the area. Gillmoss was identified, and services were transferred out leaving a depot facility and enough fleet to run the Kirkby bus routes.

In April 2000 there were major network changes that streamlined bus services on Merseyside and consolidated timetables for routes that MTL and Arriva competed on. Renumbering took place to try and have a service number used just once. Most significantly St Helens services were renumbered to 3x, Southport services to 4x, and Wirral services to 4xx. Routes moved depots too, with operational efficiencies presenting themselves based on a wider choice of depot location.

The first new buses arrived before the end of the year, with an influx of low-floor midi-buses from varying suppliers to help spread and therefore speed up the delivery time. The fleet profile has changed over the years, focussing very much on single-deck operations to begin with but gradually double-decks returned with various orders and then in 2015 there began a huge influx of larger-capacity vehicles. Looking around Liverpool City Centre today is a different sight than it was in 2010.

In terms of depots there have been changes too. In 2001 Gillmoss depot was sold to Glenvale Transport to satisfy the Monopolies and Mergers Commission. Warrington, Huyton, and Skelmersdale depots were closed in 2002, 2006, and 2011 respectively, with services transferring to other locations. St Helens depot became the company's paint and body shop when the ex-Liverline facility at Bootle was closed, and Birkenhead and Speke depots both saw significant investment and rebuilds.

In 2010 the Arriva group was purchased by the Deutsche Bahn group for around £1.5 billion. For passengers nothing noticeable changed apart from the 'a DB company' tagline appearing beneath the main Arriva logo, but with recurring intentions to sell the UK operations there are undoubtedly strategic decisions that to a degree go unnoticed by Mr Smith using service 14 five days a week to travel to work.

The purpose of this book is to show the journey that bus passengers and Arriva as a company have been on over twenty-three years on Merseyside, by looking at the changing profile of the fleet (there are some services that feature more prominently to emphasise that) and covering the transition of liveries: from the red and cream of MTL to the aquamarine and Cotswold stone of Arriva, moving to the interurban livery as standard, to the current corporate blue, and not forgetting the eco liveries thrown into the mix.

When I compiled my first book for Amberley Publishing, *Merseyside Buses 2010–2020*, I enjoyed the story that the pictures told about an industry that has been a hobby and a career. Regardless of whether either of those applies to you, there's no escaping that buses leave a mark on most of our lives (admittedly not always a positive one), but they are a marker in time of journeys to school, commutes to work, trips to the pub, the route that went past the house of a relative, or the bus you drove for some or all of your career.

All of the photos in this book have been taken by me unless credited otherwise, and I'm extremely grateful to those people for sharing those pictures with me for inclusion. I'd like to thank family, friends, and colleagues for their support and encouragement as I put this book together. On a personal level it's a homage to the MTL B10Bs and Volvo Olympians, and a salute to the Enviro400s and the buses I use on a regular basis that make travelling by public transport an enjoyable experience, and I hope that for you the reader it invokes some memories or informs you of something you didn't already know, but at the very least brings a little enjoyment as you scan through the pages.

Around 250 Leyland Titans were purchased from London Buses by MTL in the early 1990s, with many converted to single-door operation at the Edge Lane works. 2046 was twenty-one years old when the Arriva acquisition took place and is pictured in Gillmoss depot typifying the look of the MTL fleet with Arriva logo applied overnight. This bus was one of the first to leave London and also one of the last to be withdrawn, remaining in service at Gillmoss with Glenvale and then Stagecoach for another six years.

A sorry-looking line-up at Gillmoss depot, and one that was replicated in Green Lane too. Many, if not all, of the dual-door Leyland Titans were withdrawn from service quite quickly, and such was their age and condition they were cannibalised for parts rather than having any re-sale value.

Some of the Alexander-bodied Leyland Atlanteans remained in service, albeit in quickly reducing numbers, mainly at Southport and Birkenhead depots. 1007 is seen on New Brighton promenade long before the redevelopment work, and has had fleet plates removed and new fleet number 3007 applied with transfers.

Optare Metrorider 7806 was new to Merseybus in 1993 and was an early repaint into Arriva livery.

Arriva wasted no time in ordering new buses to modernise the aging fleet, and many of the first arrivals were low-floor Plaxton Pointer 2-bodied Dennis Darts. 2215 is seen here at the Albert Dock. These were part of the single-deck transition on Merseyside, with double-deck Atlanteans, Titans, and Olympians replaced with lower-capacity single-deck vehicles.

Wright Cadet-bodied DAF SB120s helped spread the new bus order, with the batch split between Birkenhead and Speke depots. 2426 went to the latter and was branded for the 80/80A where they spent nearly all of their operational life.

A lesser number of Alexander ALX200-bodied Dennis Darts also made up the new deliveries for Arriva Merseyside. Initially they went to Speke depot for the 75 and 78 Halewood routes, but after a relatively short time transferred to Bootle depot. 2263 is seen leaving Paradise Street bus station, the predecessor to Liverpool ONE bus station.

The arrival of new Scanias at Runcorn depot had seen the Plaxton Verde-bodied Dennis Lances transfer to Bootle depot to replace Leyland Nationals on service 60 between Bootle and Aigburth, a route that MTL and Arriva had long competed on. When the timetables were amalgamated in April 2000, the route allocation became a mix of Lances and B10Bs. As a regular user of the service then, this proved not to be a fun game of roulette!

A repainted Wright Endurance-bodied Volvo B10B travels along a snowy Queens Drive. A total of 120 of these perfect examples of a bus arrived in the MTL fleet between 1994 and 1996 and would operate out of all the Merseyside depots with the exception of Birkenhead.

In 2001 came the next influx of deliveries, and as part of these low-floor vehicles were introduced onto service 86 between Liverpool and Garston. Allocated to Speke depot, Wright Renown-bodied Volvo B10B 2720 is seen arriving into Paradise Street bus station, which now forms part of the pedestrianised shopping area.

Green Lane also received an allocation of the new B10Bs for service 14 between Liverpool and Croxteth, a route that had been transferred out of Gillmoss in advance of the sale. 2729 is travelling through Liverpool City Centre's other bus station, Queen Square.

As well as the B10Bs, Speke depot received more full-length single-deck vehicles in the form of East Lancs Myllenium-bodied DAF SB220s, and theirs were branded for and allocated to service 81/81A between Bootle and Speke or Liverpool John Lennon Airport, where 2471 is seen about to load. Birkenhead depot received an allocation for service 410 New Brighton to Clatterbridge.

New to Kentish Bus is 1989. Alexander-bodied Volvo Citybuses found their way to Southport depot where the batch operated on schools and service 300 Southport to Liverpool. For a time the Esplanade car park at Southport was used to park vehicles in between school duties rather than travel back to the depot at Canning Road.

When Gillmoss depot was sold to Glenvale in 2001 the Northern Counties Palatine II-bodied Volvo Olympians, new in 1998, were transferred out to be retained by Arriva, with the allocation split between Green Lane and Speke depots. 3336 is seen in the ex-Liverline yard in Bootle having been prepped for repaint.

Inside the paint shop is former Fareway Leyland Olympian 160. Alongside it is one of the DAFDB250s that had transferred up from Arriva London, and the finished result can be seen in the next photograph.

Although service 86 had new low-floor buses, the consolidation of the competing Arriva and MTL timetables soon led to capacity constraints. So, in 2001, thirteen Northern Counties-bodied DAF DB250s arrived from London and were repainted and route branded.

Alexander ALX300-bodied DAF SB220s transferred to the Merseyside fleet from Arriva Manchester and split between Green Lane and Birkenhead depots. 2412 is seen at Chester Bus Exchange, route branded for service 401 between New Brighton and Chester.

In 1995/96 MTL had taken delivery of thirty-six long wheel-based Northern Counties Palatine II-bodied Volvo Olympians, with high interior spec for use on the high-profile cross-river services between Wirral and Liverpool City Centre (apart from three that went to Southport depot). These still had plenty of quality to give Arriva and 3305 is seen leaving Liverpool City Centre for West Kirby. While route branding falls in and out of favour for all of the normal reasons, the vehicles used on the cross-river routes have consistently carried it.

Ex-MTL/Merseybus Alexander-bodied Leyland Olympian 3221 is pictured fresh from the paint shop.

A fine line-up of ex-MTL B10Bs is seen here in the layover area at Paradise Street bus station.

The Sefton Council contract for the Southport Park & Ride services transferred from MTL to Arriva, and at that time was being operated by gas-powered Plaxton Pointer 2-bodied Dennis Darts. 6249 is pictured inside Southport depot.

This book started with one of the oldest buses in service, but open-top Leyland Atlantean 1449 was even older, though duties were limited to seasonal work and football parades. Painted into corporate colours, it remained allocated to Southport depot and is now in preservation.

Volvo Olympian M218 YKC was new to Liverbus and then acquired by MTL, and when it became part of the Arriva fleet it was renumbered from 1218 to 3338. Allocated to Speke depot, it is seen here outside Liverpool University Guild of Students on service 699, which offered a frequent link between the halls of residence and the university campus.

Also outside the university is 3260, new to Merseybus in 1989 as 260, a Northern Counties-bodied Leyland Olympian. This example graduated to become a playbus in Wales.

The New Year's Day bus network has always been an important one but never the most commercial, and in some years produced some unusual workings from different depots on other operators' routes. One of the new Dennis Darts, wrapped in a Travelsafe branding, waits in the layover area of Paradise Street bus station to operate a Glenvale route, 17C.

A snow-free shot of a Plaxton Verde-bodied Dennis Lance, this time 1205, as it arrives at Bootle bus station. I always had mixed feelings about these: nice and spacious on the inside but very rattly and jerky – perhaps better suited to limited-stop work. Soon these would be replaced as the 60 became another service struggling with capacity.

When the Wright Axcess Ultralow-bodied Scania L113s transferred to Green Lane depot from Gillmoss along with service 12/13 that they had been bought by MTL for, they lost their branding on repaint but throughout their operational life it was rare to see one appear on another route.

In the layover area of Bootle bus station one of the short ex-MTL Dennis Darts is parked alongside an East Lancs-bodied Dennis Dart that had been the backbone of the North Western CityPlus fleet. Everyone has their own opinion, and in many ways there is no right or wrong, but I have no nice words to say about these, other than they're no longer in service.

Merseytravel/Merseybus had taken delivery of the first low-floor buses in the country back in 1994: 12 Neoplan N4016s. They had initially operated on the SMART network of routes, but when that contract was won by Arriva, the buses had been painted into MTL red and cream and allocated to service 18A between Liverpool City Centre and Croxteth Park. They continued to do so with Arriva until being replaced by Pulsars in 2008.

There were also some baby Neoplans. M302YBG was a Neoplan N4009, and spent several years operating one of the many incarnations of the Liverpool City Centre circular shuttle services.

6793 was part of a batch of four Ikarus-bodied DAF SB220s that were originally owned by Merseytravel but operated by Merseybus on route 224, an early version of the SMART network. These were replaced with the arrival of the Neoplans and moved to Birkenhead depot where they were allocated to services 487/488. An unusual vehicle type for MTL, but a common chassis type when in the Arriva fleet.

Dennis Dart 2221 waits on the alighting stop at Old Roan Interchange ready to depart back towards Liverpool City Centre.

With the purchase of MTL came not just buses but also the operation of the Merseyrail franchise. Some of the MTL Olympians were used as a dedicated rail replacement resource. F266 YTJ was one of these and is parked near to Hall Road station in Crosby during planned engineering works.

New to Liverbus in 1993 as part of a batch of eight and numbered 104 before being renumbered to 6904 when acquired by MTL, this Huyton depot-allocated Northern Counties Paladin-bodied Volvo B10B is arriving at Queen Square bus station. It would later transfer to Arriva Midlands.

In 2003 Arriva launched the 'Le Bus' concept following the announcement that Liverpool would be the European Capital of Culture in 2008. The initial press release referenced twenty-five branded buses on routes to Crosby and Netherton, but over the next couple of years the route coverage was spread wider. 'Le Bus' would be high frequency and high quality with audio-visual next-stop information. Alexander ALX200-bodied Dennis Dart 2269 is at Bootle Strand branded for service 52 between Liverpool City Centre and Netherton.

Plaxton Pointer 2-bodied Dennis Dart 2218 was one of the vehicles branded for service 55 between Liverpool City Centre and Old Roan, seen here pulling into Bootle bus station on diversion due to a closure of Stanley Road.

'Le Bus' came to the 12/13 Liverpool City Centre to Stockbridge Village route. These Scanias already had some of the required technology having been delivered with the equipment to transmit real-time information.

The Neoplans on service 18A also received 'Le Bus' branding.

The 14A and 14B (the Kirkby extensions of the 14 route) received the 'Le Bus' treatment on some ex-Arriva Medway Dennis Darts.

The Wright Renown-bodied Volvo B10Bs at Speke depot were branded for Le 79.

Northern Counties Palatine-bodied Volvo Olympian N706TPK spent some time at Huyton depot. It was new to Southend Transport, which became Arriva Southend. Later it would move to Arriva Midlands.

Two ex-MTL B10Bs head from James Street onto Lord Street commencing their outward journeys from Liverpool City Centre.

Capacity issues on service 60, particularly at school times, saw the B10B and Lance allocation switched to double-deck, and along came some East Lancs-bodied Volvo Citybuses that had been new to London & Country in 1993. Older but bigger but better? Their stay would only last for a couple of years.

A temporary addition to the 60 capacity remedy was ECW-bodied Leyland Olympian C212GTH. Some non-Merseyside-related info: bought new for the X1 Cymru Coastline route, it was the last ex-Crosville vehicle in service with Arriva. It would be converted to open top, and is now in preservation.

G525WJF was an Alexander-bodied Leyland Olympian new to Midland Fox that found a home on Merseyside amongst the MTL Olympians. Here it departs Queen Square bus station.

When Arriva sold Gillmoss depot to Glenvale in 2001 there was a 'no competition' agreement in place, but only Arriva against Glenvale to give the new operator a chance of sustainability. Glenvale proceeded to run on the profitable Arriva services, so inevitably once the agreement expired Arriva registered on those previously protected routes. Ex-Gillmoss Volvo Olympian 3310, then at Green Lane depot, is pictured arriving in Liverpool City Centre on service 19 from Kirkby, as work is underway preparing to demolish Paradise Street bus station.

Volvo B10B 6593 had the notable smart appearance of having the 'W' painted black. This was October 2005 and, as can be seen by the vehicles either side, was not long after Stagecoach had acquired Glenvale Transport.

6617 was one of the later MTL B10B deliveries and had been at Gillmoss for use on services 53 and 55. Here it is allocated to Speke depot and making use of one of the temporary layover bays in the final couple of weeks before the bus station would close and relocate to the new Liverpool ONE facility.

Selwyns had been operating service 500 between Liverpool City Centre and Liverpool John Lennon Airport under contract to Merseytravel, but when Arriva took the decision to take it on commercially they purchased the DAFSB120s that had been running on it. X782 NWK was numbered 2479 in the Arriva Merseyside fleet.

At the same time that MTL had been taking delivery of their Palatine II-bodied Volvo Olympians Arriva had taken Palatine I examples in Wales. From 2005 they started to appear across the different Merseyside depots.

Another incarnation of a Liverpool City Centre shuttle network of routes saw six Optare Solos funded by the EU's CATCH Project (Clean Accessible Transport for Community Health). They were fitted with hybrid drives by technology company ECONO. Unfortunately the vehicles were not considered a success and were withdrawn after eighteen months. Stagecoach then acquired them and they were adapted as part of biofuel trials.

Leyland Olympian H113 GEV was new to Grey Green, then part of Arriva London. It is seen here while allocated to Birkenhead depot and filling in on cross-river duties.

This 2005 shot shows the new Liverpool ONE bus station nearing completion, with the Hilton Hotel and Merseytravel Travel Shop still under construction behind Alexander ALX300-bodied SB220 2406, one of the ex-Manchester batch now allocated to Speke depot. The new bus station replaced the Paradise Street facility as part of the transformational development of Liverpool City Centre. It would be another two-and-a-half years until the retail element would open, a factor that hampered the initial use of the bus station by passengers.

It may look like a Pulsar that would become so common on the Merseyside network, but 2800 was a Wright Eclipse-bodied Volvo B7L, seen in Huyton bus station on service 89 operating between St Helens and Liverpool John Lennon Airport. 2800 moved about a bit: new to Arriva Kent Thameside in 2001, it moved to Bolton and then went back and forth between there and St Helens.

As well as the Plaxton- and East Lancs-bodied Dennis Lances, Arriva Merseyside also took some Wright Pathfinder low-floor examples that had started off life with London & Country. 2392 is on Stanley Road in Bootle.

Although the Neoplans were the main allocation for service 18A, B10B 6571 is seen in this 2007 shot travelling through St George's Place in Liverpool City Centre.

Scania N113 DWM was new to North Western Bee Line but later moved to St Helens depot.

7549, R549 ABA, was one of MTL's low-floor Dennis Dart deliveries in 1998, seen here turning onto Victoria Street having just terminated in Queen Square bus station.

The final new buses to be purchased by MTL were seventy-five Marshall Capital-bodied Dennis Darts in 1999. 7648 was an example that transferred to Bootle depot.

P3SLT was a step-entrance Plaxton Pointer-bodied Dennis Dart that had been new to South Lancs Travel of St Helens (hence the registration plate). Although part of Arriva North West as it was operating out of the Skelmersdale depot, the route was a key one on the Merseyside network.

As a further example of the varying types of Dennis Dart that have operated for Arriva, here is another of the ex-Arriva Medway vehicles with the 'Le Bus' branding removed but still visible if you look closely enough.

In 2006 there had been a slight shift in vehicle type, and Arriva Merseyside's first low-floor double-deckers had arrived at Speke depot. Thirty Alexander ALX400-bodied Volvo B7TLs were delivered for routes 82 and 86. 4109 is passing through Garston Village, and in the background construction is underway on the site of the old Merseybus depot.

New Wright Cadet-bodied DAF SB120s had arrived in late 2005. 2518 is travelling towards Liverpool City Centre past the New Mersey Retail Park.

Volvo B7 4112 still looks shiny and new while taking layover at the Speke Morrisons bus facility.

As with most bus fleets, Arriva Merseyside took a fair share of ex-London vehicles. 4031 was originally DLA 71 with Arriva London Northern.

MTL had purchased three Alexander Strider-bodied Volvo B10Bs for their Merseyrider operation in 1994. 6301 is passing by Calderstones Park on Menlove Avenue.

Northern Counties Paladin-bodied Scania L113 was new to North Western Skelmersdale, but by 2007 had transferred to St Helens depot and is seen operating on service 39 passing through Huyton bus station on the way to Prescot, a route that didn't have long left until being withdrawn.

Liverpool City Centre has undergone so much redevelopment that sometimes you forget how things used to look. One of the oldest and one of the newest MTL B10Bs are at the Mann Island terminus with work underway in the background to redevelop the Pier Head area, including new Ferry Terminal and canal link.

When Arriva won the Merseytravel SMART contract from MTL they introduced some new low-floor Dennis Darts in a special eco livery. When Arriva commercialised the network of routes the vehicles were repainted into corporate livery. 2322 is pictured on Castle Street.

When Arriva had stopped competing with Stagecoach on the 'Glenvale routes' the half of the Volvo Olympians that had been allocated to Green Lane depot moved to Bootle depot and replaced the Citybuses on service 60. 3313 is on Ullet Road.

Two of the ALX400 Volvo B7s pass outside Liverpool ONE bus station.

As well as receiving new double-deckers, Speke depot also received some Wright Commander-bodied VDLSB200s.

The Commanders became the latest bus to be allocated and branded for service 500 to the airport. 2602 travels along Dale Street in Liverpool City Centre painted in the special Airlink livery.

The layover area at Speke Morrisions is again the location, this time for one of the Speke depot Volvo Olympians.

ALX400-bodied Volvo B7 4101 has just called at Liverpool South Parkway and is continuing on the way to Liverpool City Centre from Liverpool John Lennon Airport.

By 2007 the 'Le Bus' branding had been revised and some routes fell out and others fell in. Dennis Dart 2207 shows off the change from purple to red as it waits to leave Huyton bus station.

Wright Renown-bodied Volvo B10B 2720 makes a second appearance in this book, this time 'Le Bus' branded for the 79.

In contrast to the previous photos where the buses were branded referencing specific routes, a batch of Commanders were given a generic version to be used across the Halewood services.

Northern Counties-bodied DAF SB220 1795 spent some time allocated to Birkenhead depot in 2008. Previously it had been with Arriva Wales branded for service 11 Chester to Rhyl, and before that wore the white and green of Crosville Cymru.

The publicity of new bus arrivals varies. Some go quietly straight into service, some get a line-up for a photograph, and some get a higher-profile launch. In November 2008 when the Wright Pulsar-bodied VDL SB220s arrived at Green Lane depot to replace the Neoplans on service 18A, this photoshoot took place at Croxteth Hall with Croxteth ward councillor Rose Bailey and members of the Arriva management team. (Photo: Arriva North West)

Pulsars 2672 and 2900 are seen here in Green Lane depot.

2903 begins the circular route around Croxteth Park with snowy surroundings.

In 2009, with the cross-river Olympians fourteen years old, it was time for an upgrade, and twenty-three Enviro400-bodied Alexander Dennis Trident 2s arrived at Birkenhead depot, the first to carry the 'interurban' livery. And of course, they received route branding. 4422 is in Liverpool City Centre and preparing to depart back over to the Wirral.

N134 DWM was another Scania that had been new to North Western Bee Line, but one that transferred to Green Lane depot rather than St Helens. The Merseytravel SMART logos either side of the destination screen are from its days branded for the 320 St Helens to Ashton route.

In 2009 the 60 route changed vehicles again, this time getting twelve new Alexander Dennis Enviro400s. Unlike the cross-river deliveries, these were in standard livery and had Arriva moquette seating. 4427 loads in Bootle bus station.

A trip to Southport on a B10B was always a pleasure, particularly along the Formby bypass! 6619 was one of the ex-Gillmoss examples.

In 2009 the Pulsar deliveries switched to the newer Pulsar 2 model, the most noticeable difference being the front. 3007 went to Birkenhead depot and is pictured travelling along Woodchurch Road.

3012 was part of the Green Lane depot deliveries and prompted the next vehicle type for service 14.

3018 went to Bootle depot.

Two of the cross-river Enviro400s are pictured at Birkenhead bus station.

Step-entrance Dennis Dart P830 RWU, numbered 1330 in the Arriva North West fleet, is seen here in 2012 while allocated to Birkenhead depot about to enter Birkenhead bus station. It was new to Arriva South London and had previously been at Winsford and Hawarden depots.

The introduction of a Quality Partnership on service 10A between Arriva, Stagecoach, and Merseytravel saw the introduction of low-floor vehicles to the route. Pulsar 2 2993 loads passengers on James Street.

There were still occasions when step-entrance vehicles found their way onto the 10A allocation. New to North Western, Scania 1061, with a newly upgraded destination screen, leaves Queen Square bus station.

Although many of the cross-river Olympians were either withdrawn or displaced following the arrival of the Enviro400s, some were still in service in 2011. 3301 waits at West Kirby, and despite its age had been repainted into what had now become the standard Arriva livery.

Myllenium 2467 was repainted into the new livery and is seen away from the usual 81 route at Liverpool South Parkway.

Repaints into the new livery continued across the fleet. The MTL Scanias on the 12/13 always retained their unique split destination displays.

Route branding was rare on Arriva buses once 'Le Bus' had gone, but one of the exceptions for a time was the revised 47/48A. The new style of branding is seen here on 3041, which formed part of the 2010 delivery schedule where buses were now arriving in the interurban livery as standard.

The Grand National at Aintree Racecourse is a major event for the Liverpool City Region, with people travelling locally and from further afield to attend at least one of the three race days. It provides a commercial opportunity for shuttle services from Liverpool City Centre, and in 2011 one of the ex-Wales Volvo Olympians, 3344, leads the waiting line on Lime Street.

With the arrival of Pulsars at St Helens depot some of the step-entrance Scanias were pushed to other depots. P136 GND was an East Lancs Spryte-bodied version that went to Speke. Approaching behind is one of the amphibious tour vehicles that famously carried Queen Elizabeth II into the dock during her visit to Liverpool.

Repainted 2415, one of the ex-Manchester DAF SB220s, travels through the Liverpool University campus area.

2477 was an ex-Arriva Kent & Sussex Plaxton Prestige-bodied DAF SB220, seen here at Liverpool ONE bus station.

When articulated buses were cast out of London, ten Mercedes-Benz Citaros were transferred from Arriva London to Arriva Merseyside, all going to Speke depot. Eight were painted in standard livery and used on service 500 to the airport and service 699 to the university. 6013 DX04 MXL is at Liverpool ONE bus station.

The remaining two Citaros were painted in a revised livery for service 501 that ran between Liverpool South Parkway and Liverpool John Lennon Airport. 6014 travels along Horrocks Avenue in Garston.

In 2011 forty-four Wright Gemini 2-bodied VDL DB300s arrived at Speke depot for services 79 and 82, although 4457 found its way onto the 500 very quickly.

4467 departs Liverpool ONE bus station. The arrival of these vehicles on the 82 displaced some of the Volvo B7s to Southport depot for services 375/385 to Wigan.

The arrival of the Geminis at Speke depot meant that the Volvo Olympians had reached the stage of being 'spare' vehicles moving from depot to depot as required. 3335 transferred to Birkenhead and has just arrived in Liverpool City Centre.

The route rationalisation that took place following the acquisition of MTL saw route changes and the brave decision to renumber services to make the route numbering a lot more straightforward. A long-standing anomaly to this was the 18A; it had been quite a while since there had been just an 18, so the 'A' suggested a variant when it was in fact the only route. It took until 2012 for the 'A' to be dropped.

In March 2013 thirty-three Wright Eclipse Gemini 2-bodied Volvo B5LH electric hybrid vehicles arrived at Birkenhead depot for the cross-river services, wearing the corporate eco livery. 4516 is only a couple of days old in this shot and carries promotional advertising.

Dennis Dart S249UVR makes a second appearance but looking quite different, and not just in terms of livery. The batch of buses were repowered from gas to conventional diesel at the end of their Park & Ride contract and moved to the general fleet. It was also renumbered from 6249 to 2292. It is seen here manoeuvring in Southport town centre for a Bus Users UK event. Unfortunately it was larger than the permit allowed for the pedestrianised area and had to be quickly substituted for a Cumfybus Solo.

In the autumn of 2012 another batch of Pulsar 2s arrived across various North West depots with 3127 going to Birkenhead to replace the Myllenium DAFs. It is seen here passing Birkenhead Park heading to Clatterbridge Hospital.

Departing Mann Island in some light snow, Pulsar 2905 has been repainted into the updated livery.

In 2013 there was some swapping of vehicles due to the arrival of the Hybrids. The Enviro400s from Birkenhead were split between Bootle depot and Arriva Wales, with the latter group being refurbished to Arriva Sapphire spec for service 1 between Wrexham and Chester. Pulsar 2906 made the return journey, arriving at Birkenhead depot having previously been branded for the 1.

4419 was one of the Enviro400s that moved to Bootle depot. It is seen here with branding removed and about to turn into Broadway, Norris Green. The route of the 61 would soon be moved away from here due to the ongoing problem of double-parked cars.

The additional double-deck vehicles now at Bootle depot meant that the twelve that had been bought back in 2009 found their way onto other routes. 4428 is about to pull onto the loading stop on Sir Thomas Street in Liverpool City Centre.

Repainted Marshall-bodied Dennis Dart 7659 turns onto London Road with St George's Hall as a backdrop.

Service 14 would continue to be single-deck allocated for several more years. Pulsar 2 3066 is pictured at the driver relief point at Broadway in 2013. The bus would later move to Arriva Midlands.

Originally new to Speke depot, Wright Renown-bodied Volvo B10B 2723 transferred to Southport with the arrival of the Gemini double-decks. When repainted it regained the black 'W'.

Wright Cadet 2432 is departing Woodside to make the far from direct trip to Mill Park. The route would be withdrawn in 2017 as part of the Wirral area network review when it was considered no longer commercially viable.

January 2015 marked the start of the double-decker influx. In the space of a year 128 Alexander Dennis Enviro400s would arrive for Bootle, Green Lane, Southport, Speke, and St Helens depots. Thirty-six arrived for the 10, 10A and 10B Prescot Road routes. 4584 was one of Green Lane's.

4622 was one of sixteen 'Posh & Double Decks' that arrived at Bootle depot for the 52, 52A routes.

4656 arrived at Green Lane depot in the summer, with West Derby Road routes 12, 13, and 15 moving to double-deck allocation.

The new buses carried varying promotional advertising such as '50% more bus 100% more luxury', shouting about the fact that there was more capacity but also highlighting a step change in vehicle specification with higher-quality seating and free WiFi.

It wasn't just double-deck vehicles that arrived in 2015. Birkenhead depot received six Wright StreetLite DF buses, originally intended for service 487 but seen here in Birkenhead bus station on the 410.

Vehicles old and new can be seen in this 2015 shot of Victoria Street in Liverpool City Centre. New Enviro400 4658 is about to travel round to Queen Square bus station, East Lancs Myllenium DAF 2463 is on a layover stand, while one of the cross-river Hybrids loads on the bus stop behind.

St Helens depot had two types of Optare Solo. One of the 'classic' examples was 680, waiting to depart St Helens bus station on cross-town service 35 from Gillars Green.

Arriva had added to their North West portfolio in 2005 by purchasing Blue Bus of Bolton. Y36 KNB was an Ikarus Polaris-bodied DAF SB220 bought new by Blue Bus and had a short stay at Green Lane towards the end of its days. Very few of this type were actually imported into the UK.

One of the St Helens depot-allocated Enviro400s was 4596, loading in St Helens bus station in 2016.

The arrival of the new Enviro400s at Speke depot for service 86 coincided with the withdrawal of the Myllenium DAFs on service 81, so the remaining B7s brought some additional capacity (and quality). 4112 is seen here on Queens Drive in Walton, and wears a vinyl poppy that is applied across the fleet in November.

In late 2016 and 2017 fifty-one new double-deck vehicles arrived, this time more Hybrids but now Euro 6. Low-height Wright Gemini 3-bodied Volvo B5LH buses were split between Green Lane and Speke depots, but before entering general service the 2016 batch spent several months on rail replacement work while the Merseyrail loop line was closed for slab track-replacement work. 4802 is pictured outside the Liverpool City Region Combined Authority offices at Mann Island. As well as the free WiFi and environmental benefits, the vehicles also offered USB charging in all of the seatbacks.

With the closure of the loop line so significant, it was not just a fleet of buses to move passengers that was required. Many people take their bicycles on the rail network, the River Mersey proving an obstacle. Therefore B10B 8214 (previously 6514) was taken from the driver training fleet and converted to be a 'Rail Replacement Bike Bus', with space and fixtures provided to accommodate bikes. (Photo: Karl Wilton)

In the autumn of 2017 to mark the anniversary of the Merseyside Bus Alliance a number of buses gathered at the Pier Head. 4850, one of the Speke-allocated Hybrids, was in attendance.

Although technically an Arriva North West bus, due to being allocated to Runcorn depot, the gas-powered Caetano-bodied MAN Ecocity would be a regular sight on the routes coming into Liverpool. These zero-emission buses saw the introduction of a revised corporate eco livery.

The Alexander Dennis Enviro400mmc became a common sight on Merseyside with the number that Stagecoach took, but Arriva took just five as part of the next double-deck deliveries after the Hybrids, and had standard Euro6 engines. They also marked the first double-deck buses to arrive in the new corporate light-blue livery.

2017 saw two different types of zero-emission deliveries. Runcorn depot took the gas buses and Green Lane depot took twelve Enviro200mmc-bodied BYD electric buses for the 26/27 Sheil Road Circular route.

Pulsar 2 3018 arrives in Liverpool City Centre from Skelmersdale.

Hybrid 4846 negotiates a slalom of traffic management as it travels through the works being carried out on Victoria Street as part of Liverpool City Council's Connectivity scheme. There were regular phases of these works that would leave buses with inches of room and the tightest of tight manoeuvres.

Generations meet at Mann Island, as a Hybrid pulls past preserved Liverpool Corporation AEC Regent III A36. (Photo: Karl Wilton)

Covid-19 had a big impact on bus services, as it did on so many things. A night shot of 4593 on Corporation Street in St Helens shows the 'please wear a face covering on board' message on the destination blind, which would alternate between the route's destination.

With social-distancing rules significantly reducing the capacity on buses, there came a problem in September 2020 when schools reopened. DfE guidance allowed 'closed'-school services to operate at full capacity due to schoolchildren being considered to be in bubbles and making the same journeys each day. Across the Merseyside network where data showed high volumes of school travel, duplicate journeys were introduced to ensure there remained sufficient capacity on the network for key-worker travel. 4569 travels along Queens Drive on an S81A.

From 2020 buses in Liverpool City Centre had the use of a designated layover area on Old Haymarket on the site of a former pay & display car park. It was created as part of the City Centre Bus Re-routing that saw most services curtailed at Queen Square bus station, which meant there needed to be layover spaces provided for buses to wait time between journeys. Eight spaces were provided as well as some on Victoria Street, but crucially at Old Haymarket there were driver facilities.

Bootle depot's 4420 carries the colours of the Pride flag, and in 2020 had the dedication to key workers added to the nearside advertising space.

In 2020 service 500 had a facelift and was rebranded. Arriving at Liverpool ONE bus station, 4477 was one of three Wright Gemini 2s painted into a more striking special livery.

One of the BYD electric buses arrives at Liverpool ONE bus station on an unusual allocation on service 18.

As part of the work to 'support' Liverpool City Council's Connectivity scheme, how buses travelled around the city centre changed in January 2021. The 7 was a route that moved bus stations from Queen Square to Liverpool ONE. 3061 is the lead of no fewer than six buses arriving from Hanover Street.

The Hybrids at Birkenhead depot began to be repainted into the new Arriva eco livery. 4502 calls at Arrowe Park Hospital interchange.

The Volvo B7s continued to find themselves in service despite their age. 4115 had moved to Birkenhead depot and is ready to depart on a 464 to New Ferry.

Optare Solo SR 721 passes in front of St Helens Town Hall.

The old and the new eco liveries are seen together at the Cook Street layover stands.

In January 2022 twenty-four integral Wright StreetDecks were delivered to Green Lane depot for services 10B and 14. They were Euro6 and had on-board audio-visual next-stop announcements, the first since the 'Le Bus' programme. Along with some new vehicles in Southport, they represented an investment of £7.4 million by Arriva. 4719 is pictured at the Willow Way terminus in Croxteth on the first weekend of service.

4712 is pictured at the Old Haymarket layover area waiting time before departing to Huyton.

The Southport depot vehicles that formed part of that £7.4 million investment were 10 Wright StreetLites for local services. 6010 shows off its newness. (Photo: Ray Dobson)

Enviro400 4651 loads at Queen Square bus station.

Another night shot, this time of Wright Pulsar 2 3040 on evening layover at Old Haymarket.

Similar to the Enviro400mmc, the Enviro200 is a common sight across the country but not for Arriva on Merseyside. Four were purchased for the Southport Park & Ride contract and were later joined by another four ex-London examples. 2163 had transferred to Birkenhead depot following the arrival at Southport of some new StreetLites, and here makes an unusual appearance on service 437.

New in 2006, so into its sixteenth year of service, Wright Commander-bodied VDLSB220 passes St Helens Town Hall in 2022.

On a sunny summer's day the Green Lane and Speke Hybrids line up nicely as they load passengers in Liverpool ONE bus station. Though not quite clear in the background, on one of the layover stands is a 2013 Gemini 2-bodied Volvo B5LH that had transferred from Manchester to Speke depot.

To celebrate the Queen's Platinum Jubilee in 2022 Southport-allocated Enviro400 4579 was given a commemorative livery.

An Arriva line-up at the annual open day of the North West Vehicle Restoration Trust, Kirkby, in 2022. Left to right: Speke depot's 500 branded Gemini 2 4477, Bootle depot's Enviro400mmc 4696, Southport depot's Enviro400 4579, Birkenhead depot's Hybrid 4509, and Green Lane depot's StreetDeck 4733.

Sometimes things come full circle. CX55 AEO was new to Speke depot as 4105. It would later transfer to Southport for routes 375 and 385 before moving on to Winsford depot. On withdrawal from public service it entered the driver training fleet as 8300 and returned back to Speke depot.

Wright Commander-bodied VDL SB200 started off with Arriva Wales before transferring to Speke then Bootle then into the driver training fleet where it was renumbered to 8270.

Although some of the oldest buses in the fleet, the original Pulsars continue to be repainted into the new livery. 2697 is seen in October 2022.

To mark Remembrance Sunday most Arriva buses receive a small poppy on their front, but Birkenhead depot's 4510 carries an all-over design for the British Legion.

Allocated to Southport depot, where this photo was taken, Enviro400 4580 also carries the poppy design. (Photo: Ray Dobson)

Here we see the 2022 Christmas message displayed on the destination blinds.

There were some glimpses of this part of Lime Street in other photos, but the junction in front of the station entrance has changed quite significantly from what it was. A couple of St Helens-allocated Enviro400s arrive at dusk.

At Newton-le-Willows Interchange two Pulsar 2s on service 34 meet: one is on the way to St Helens and the other to Leigh.

A subtle shot of Arriva's dominance in Liverpool City Centre. Enviro400 4615 takes layover on Crosshall Street after arriving from St Helens.

In early 2023 Bootle depot took delivery of nine MCV eVoRa-bodied Volvo B8RLEs as part of a batch split between Merseyside and Wales. 3196 is in Queen Square bus station.

The route of the 699 extends from Mount Pleasant down into the city centre of an evening and of a weekend. 4446 passes through the Adelphi junction with destination blind already set for the return journey.

The 26/27 route had had the new electric vehicles bought for it back in 2017 but capacity and range issues saw double-deck allocations become more and more common. Enviro400 4674 leads a Hybrid through Liverpool City Centre.

Repainted Optare Solo SR 715 is seen here taking layover on Corporation Street, St Helens, before it would depart on a 33 to Sutton Heath.

A not too dissimilar picture to earlier on of Victoria Street, as one of the new MCV eVoRas passes an Enviro400 and Hybrid taking layover.

Even though they no longer operate the Merseyrail franchise, Arriva hold the Merseyrail rail replacement contract, and buses can come from all depots to cover the work. Bootle-allocated 4429 arrives at Moorfields station during engineering work on the Kirkby line.

I could be wrong, but I don't recall Arriva Merseyside ever operating a dual-door bus on Merseyside (other than the short-lived dual-doored Leyland Titans in 2000, but those doors were not operational). The exception is LJ08 CYH, new to Arriva London as T55, becoming 4699 in the Arriva North West fleet when it transferred up in summer 2021, initially to Winsford but then to Bootle. It has retained the centre doors and is primarily an auxiliary vehicle being used for bus tests, driver training and rail-replacement work. It is seen here at Maghull station testing out the roads around Maghull for overhanging trees ahead of some rail-replacement duties. (Photo: Barry Dobson)

Same shell, different underneath! Broadly speaking, anyhow. A Euro6 diesel alongside a Euro6 electric hybrid.

Arriva operate the internal Aintree Racecourse shuttle during the Grand National event. In 2023 the new eVoRas were used and as night sets in 3195 poses in front of the Lord Sefton and Earl of Derby Stands. (Photo: Ray Dobson)

Although the ten Wright StreetLites were delivered to Southport depot in January 2022, following Merseytravel contract gains elsewhere, 6011 was one of four that transferred to Speke depot in 2023. It is seen here at Liverpool John Lennon Airport about to depart on a 3A journey to Huyton.

The Eurovision Song Contest came to Liverpool in May 2023, and the city embraced the competition and the thousands of visitors that came to enjoy the two-week festival. Both Arriva and Stagecoach wrapped an Enviro400mmc in an eye-catching design. 4693 was the Arriva vehicle, seen here heading to the musically appropriate Penny Lane. Bus stepped up when it needed to, with extra services and night bus journeys ensuring nobody was left behind.

With Eurovision fever having moved on to Swedish preparations, 4693 had the overall wrap removed and replaced with an updated version of the Zoe's Place Baby Hospice wrap that Enviro400 4426 had carried for nearly ten years (see *Merseyside Buses 2010–2020*). Zoe's Place is Arriva Merseyside's corporate charity and the new-look bus was unveiled at their charity golf tournament in July 2023. The annual tournament has raised almost £300,000 for Zoe's Place, which provides palliative, respite, and end-of-life care to children from birth to five years old who are suffering from life-limiting or life-threatening conditions. (Photo: Ray Dobson)

Twenty Alexander Dennis Enviro400FCEV hydrogen-fuelled vehicles were purchased by Liverpool City Region Combined Authority and then leased to Arriva and to Stagecoach for use on service 10A between Liverpool and St Helens. As well as being zero-emission vehicles, the internal specification is the highest there has been for new buses on Merseyside, with bespoke oquette and coving designs, USB charging and mobile-device holders on the seatbacks, audio-visual next-stop announcements, and much more. (Photo: Patrick Warner)

Wright StreetDeck 4712 turns into Castle Street on the morning peak extension to service 14, with Liverpool Town Hall looking quite imposing in the background. Castle Street becomes a pedestrianised area throughout the day, and the barrier blocks were painted blue and yellow as part of hosting Eurovision on behalf of Ukraine in 2023.

Normal allocations are switched in this picture, with Enviro400 4657 on service 14 laying over in Liverpool City Centre as Wright StreetDeck 4730 manoeuvres out to head to Queen Square bus station to commence service 15.

On a wet October morning Pulsar 2 3162 has sneaked onto service 18's allocation.

This book started with a bus that was twenty-one years old and ends with a picture of one of the Hybus vehicles in service. Note the revised operator logos from the earlier shot. 4900 is heading back to St Helens where the ten Arriva vehicles were allocated.